THE *Connecticut* COLONY

Our Thirteen Colonies

SPIRIT
of America®

THE *Connecticut* COLONY

By Michael Burgan

Content Adviser: Marla Miller, Ph.D. Director, Public History Program,
University of Massachusetts, Amherst, Massachusetts

The Child's World®
Chanhassen, Minnesota

9

THE *Connecticut* COLONY

Published in the United States of America by The Child's World®
PO Box 326 • Chanhassen, MN 55317-0326 • 800-599-READ • www.childsworld.com

Acknowledgments
The Child's World®: Mary Berendes, Publishing Director

Editorial Directions, Inc.: E. Russell Primm, Editorial Director; Melissa McDaniel, Line Editor; Elizabeth K. Martin, Assistant Editor; Olivia Nellums, Editorial Assistant; Susan Hindman, Copy Editor; Joanne Mattern, Proofreader; Kevin Cunningham, Peter Garnham, Ruthanne Swiatkowski, Fact Checkers; Tim Griffin/IndexServ, Indexer; Cian Loughlin O'Day, Photo Researcher; Linda S. Koutris, Photo Selector

Photo
Cover: North Wind Picture Archives; Art Resource, New York: 35; Bettmann/Corbis: 31, 32; Bridgeman Art Library: 10, 20 (Free Art Library, Philadelphia), 30; Corbis: 6 (The Mariner's Museum), 11 (Raymon Gehman), 14 (Lee Snider; Lee Snider), 19 (Historical Picture Archive), 21 (The Burstein Collection), 26, 27 (Richard Cummins); Getty Images/Hulton Archive: 9, 23, 25; North Wind Picture Archives: 8, 12, 13, 15, 16, 17, 18, 22, 28, 29-top, 29-bottom; Stock Montage: 34.

Library of Congress Cataloging-in-Publication Data
Burgan, Michael.
  The Connecticut colony / by Michael Burgan.
    p. cm. — (Our colonies)
"Spirit of America."
Includes bibliographical references (p.) and index.
Contents: The Algonquians of Connecticut—Exploration and settlement—Becoming a colony—Connecticut during the war—After the war and nationhood—Time line—Glossary terms.
  ISBN 1-56766-609-4 (alk. paper)
  1. Connecticut—History—Colonial period, ca. 1600–1775—Juvenile literature. 2. Connecticut—History—1775–1865—Juvenile literature. [1. Connecticut—History—Colonial period, ca. 1600–1775. 2. Connecticut—History—1775–1865.] I. Title. II. Series.
  F97.B886 2003
  974.6'02—dc21   2003003600

Contents

Chapter ONE

The Algonquians of Connecticut

A picture of two Algonquian chiefs from the 16th century

MORE THAN 10,000 YEARS AGO, NATIVE AMERI-cans began to settle in what is now Connecticut. By the time Europeans reached North America, a group of Native Americans called the Algonquians lived in the New England region. They belonged to many different communities, but they shared a similar language. The Algonquians of Connecticut included the Pequot, Mohegan, Niantic, Podunk, and Nipmuc.

The name *Connecticut* comes from an Algonquian word meaning "along the long tidal river." This name refers to New England's longest river, which runs through the middle of Connecticut and drains

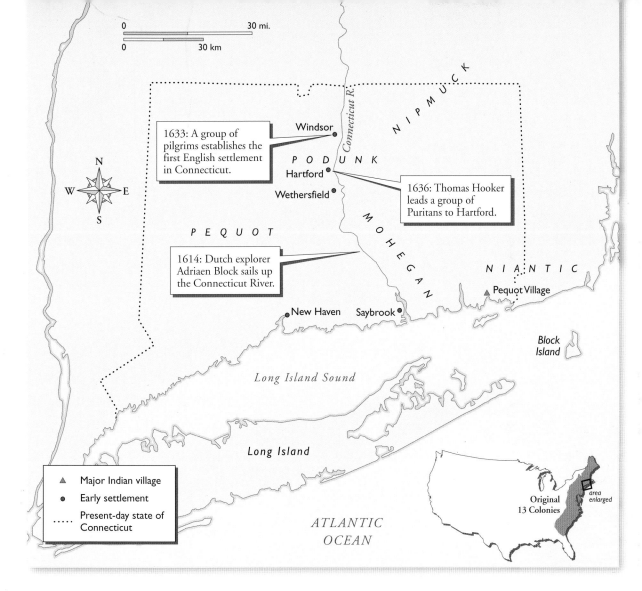

0   30 mi.

0   30 km

N I P M U C K

Windsor

1633: A group of pilgrims establishes the first English settlement in Connecticut.

P O D U N K

Hartford

Wethersfield

1636: Thomas Hooker leads a group of Puritans to Hartford.

P E Q U O T

1614: Dutch explorer Adriaen Block sails up the Connecticut River.

M O H E G A N

Connecticut R.

N I A N T I C

Pequot Village

New Haven   Saybrook

Block Island

N
W   E
S

Long Island Sound

Long Island

▲   Major Indian village
●   Early settlement
.....   Present-day state of Connecticut

Original 13 Colonies

area enlarged

ATLANTIC OCEAN

into Long Island Sound. It is a tidal river because its water rises and falls with the tides of Long Island Sound.

The people of Connecticut hunted, fished, and farmed to support their communities. Each tribe usually split up into smaller groups, called bands. Most lived along the coast or river shores. They often moved between one area where they farmed and another where they hunted. Men

Connecticut Colony at the time of the first European settlement

7

▶ The Pequot were the most powerful of the native peoples of Connecticut. In the early 17th century, some Pequots split away from the main group and called themselves the Mohegan. James Fenimore Cooper wrote about this tribe in his famous book, *The Last of the Mohicans* (Mohegans are also called Mohicans.)

hunted a variety of animals and birds, including deer, rabbits, turkeys, and ducks. Some animals, such as wolves and foxes, were prized for their fur. In the waters, the Algonquians snared sturgeon, salmon, and other fish. Close to shore, women and children helped gather shellfish.

Women did the farming for the Algonquian tribes. Their main crop was corn, but they also raised beans and squash. The women used sticks, stones, and bones to hoe the earth. (Most Algonquian tools were made of wood, bone, or stone. They did not have iron or other metals.) Children helped their mothers by gathering wild berries and nuts. The Algonquian women also built the homes in the community, called wigwams. These dome-shaped buildings

Algonquians lived in sturdy wigwams that were easy to move from place to place.

were made of wooden poles covered with bark or animal skins. The women built a fire inside the wigwam for cooking and heat. Smoke left the home through a hole in the roof.

The leaders of Algonquian bands were called sachems. The chief sachems had several other sachems below them in power. The chief sachems' duties included assigning land for farming and settling arguments between band members. The sachems also dealt with the leaders of other bands. Another important person in Algonquian life was the shaman, who served as both a religious leader and a doctor.

For the most part, the Algonquian tribes of Connecticut lived peacefully together. Their greatest threat came from the Mohawk, an Iroquois tribe from New York. The Mohawk hunted in western Connecticut and prevented Algonquian tribes from settling in that region. Tribes near the Mohawk hunting grounds had to pay **tribute** to keep the

Interesting Fact

▶ In addition to Connecticut, the states of Missouri, Michigan, and Mississippi may all derive their place names from the Algonquian language.

A shaman was the religious leader and doctor for the Algonquian tribe.

Many Native American tribes got along well with the first European settlers, trading goods and sharing the land peacefully.

peace. The other major military power was the Pequot. This Algonquian tribe lived in southeastern Connecticut, near the shore.

When Europeans came to Connecticut in the early 1600s, some Algonquians welcomed them. They hoped these settlers would help protect them from their enemies, the Mohawk and the Pequot. Many of the tribes and the Europeans got along well. They traded goods and lived near each other with no problems. The Europeans, however, brought new diseases that the Native Americans could not fight, and many thousands died from these illnesses.

FOR THE ALGONQUIANS OF CONNECTICUT, FIRE WAS A USEFUL TOOL. TO BUILD their canoes, called dugouts, men would first cut down a tree. Then they would remove the center of that tree by chopping and burning it. It was easier to scrape the center out when it had burned. This area became the inside of the canoe, where passengers could sit.

The Algonquians set fires to clear land for planting. They also set them in forests beyond their farmlands. Usually set twice a year, in spring and fall, these

fires destroyed dead trees and plants, while leaving most of the tall, healthy trees alone. Some of these surviving trees provided nuts gathered for food.

After the fires, new grass and plants sprouted on the forest's floor, attracting hungry deer the Algonquians could hunt. The fires made the hunters' job easier by clearing out trees or bushes that might hide the deer from their view. The flames also killed insects that carried diseases harmful to both humans and animals.

Chapter TWO

European Exploration and Settlement

Captain Adriaen Block and his crew building the Restless

IN 1614, DUTCH SEA CAPTAIN ADRIAEN BLOCK left the island now known as Manhattan on a ship he and his crew had built, named *Restless*. The Dutch had been exploring New York's Hudson River area for several years. Block's voyage took him across Long Island Sound to the Connecticut River. He sailed up the river to what is now Hartford (the capital of Connecticut). Block was the first European to explore that region. He saw Algonquian villages along the river, and he thought the Dutch could trade with them for furs. About 7,000 Algonquians lived near the river at this time.

Officials in Holland waited several years before sending anyone back to Connecticut. During the 1620s, the Dutch set up a small trading post at the mouth of the Connecticut River. In 1633, Dutch traders bought land from the Pequot in Hartford and set up a small fort.

Soon, the Dutch had neighbors along the river. Earlier, in 1632, Edward Winslow had sailed up the Connecticut. Winslow was one of the Pilgrim settlers in Plymouth, Massachusetts. He returned to Plymouth and described the excellent farmland that bordered the Connecticut River. In the fall of 1633, a group of Pilgrims reached what is now Windsor, just north of Hartford. They set up a small house they had brought with them from Plymouth and built a fort around it. This settlement was the first English town in Connecticut.

Soon other groups of English settlers came to Connecticut from Massachusetts. Some settled in what is now Wethersfield, just south of Hartford. Others founded the town of Saybrook, at the mouth of the Connecticut River. A group of Puritans led by well-known minister Thomas Hooker settled along the river in Hartford. They were to have the biggest effect on the formation of the colony.

Thomas Hooker was the leader of a group of Puritans from Massachusetts that settled along the river in present-day Hartford.

Interesting Fact

▶ Adriaen Block and his crew had to build the *Restless* after a fire destroyed their previous ship, the *Tiger*. Captain and crew were stranded on Manhattan Island for the winter until they launched their new vessel in the spring of 1614.

The first Puritans in America had settled in the area around Boston, Massachusetts. They shared some of the religious beliefs of the Pilgrims. Both of these **Protestant** groups had come to America to worship as they chose. They did not want to follow the rules of the main religion in England, which was the Church of England. The Puritans and Pilgrims believed people should closely follow the teachings in the Bible. They also said worshippers should form their own church communities, called congregations, and choose their own ministers.

In 1636, Hooker led a congregation of about 100 men, women, and children from the Boston area to Hartford. Hooker had disagreements with the leaders in Massachusetts and wanted to start his own Puritan community in Connecticut. Two years later, another group of Puritans settled in New Haven, on the shore of Long Island Sound. New Haven, like Saybrook, acted independently from the three "River Towns" of Hartford, Windsor, and Wethersfield.

In 1637, the River Towns joined together, partly out of self-defense, as they faced a war with the Pequot. The same year, the General Court for the River Towns met in Hartford for the first time. The court was the government for the Connecticut Colony, with representatives from each town serving on it.

Puritans celebrate their first Sunday in New Haven, Connecticut.

In 1638, Hooker called on the settlers to write down basic rules for their government. He said the people of the community had the right to choose their own leaders. The leaders' power to govern depended on the permission of the voters. Hooker's ideas formed the basis of the **Fundamental** Orders, which were approved in 1639. This document described the government and methods for voting. Some historians call the Fundamental Orders an early example of a **constitution,** like the one that created the U.S. government of today.

Trouble with the Pequot began almost as soon as the English settled in Connecticut. In 1636, John Oldham, one of the founders of Wethersfield, was sailing in Long Island Sound. His boat was attacked by Native Americans from Block Island, and the killers fled to the Pequot fort near Saybrook. Puritans from Massachusetts went to the Pequot village, seeking the murderers. The English forces destroyed wigwams, canoes, and crops. Angry Pequot warriors struck back by attacking the English fort in Saybrook. Feeling they were in danger, too, the three River Towns organized a force of 90 soldiers to attack the Pequot. Mohegan and Narragansett warriors joined this small army, as the Pequot were also their enemy.

Captain John Mason led the settlers and their Native American allies. On May 26, 1637, the soldiers set fire to the Pequot fort, then waited for the people inside to flee the flames. Most of them, however, could not escape. As Mason later wrote, "Thus in little more than one hour's space was their . . . fort with themselves utterly destroyed, to the number of six or seven hundred." The dead included many women and children. The Pequot who survived the fire were sent to live with the Mohegan and other nearby tribes or were sent into slavery.

The Pequot War ended the main American Indian threat to the Connecticut settlers. Today, the Pequot call the war a massacre, one that almost completely wiped out their people.

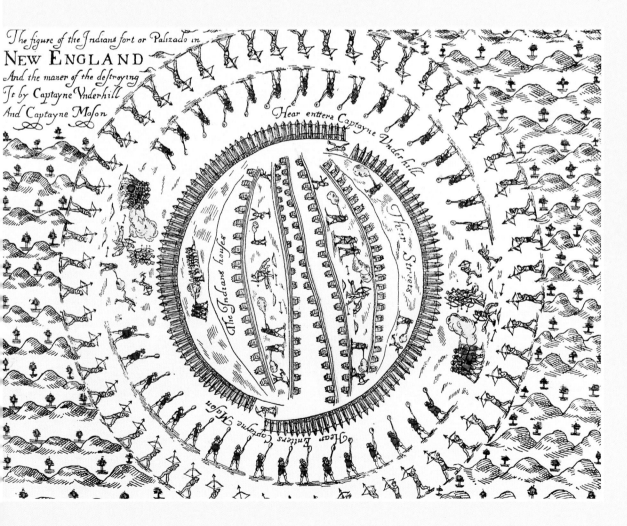

Chapter THREE

Becoming a Colony

IN 1644, SAYBROOK JOINED THE RIVER TOWNS as part of the Connecticut Colony. Several other towns also joined, though New Haven remained independent. The Fundamental Orders remained the basic outline of the government, with the General Court handling daily affairs. In 1650, the colonists wrote down a new set of laws, called the Code of 1650. The laws were largely based on the Bible. Citizens could be put to death for such crimes as murder, kidnapping, and worshipping any god other than the Christian God.

Citizens of Connecticut discuss the laws that will govern their colony.

Adult males were required to own guns to help protect against Native American attacks.

Although the colonists were far from Eng-

18

land, events there affected their lives. A few years after the founding of the Connecticut Colony, Puritans took control of the English government. They won a war that ended the rule of King Charles I. The Connecticut settlers believed England's new Puritan leaders would never challenge their control of the colony.

Charles II became the king of England in 1660.

In 1660, however, the Puritans were forced out of power in England, and King Charles II took the throne. The Connecticut settlers, most of whom had moved to Connecticut from the Massachusetts Bay Colony, knew their colony was now at risk. Without the king's permission, they had no legal right to control the colony. In 1661, Connecticut governor John Winthrop Jr. traveled to England to obtain a **charter** for his colony. A respected politician and scientist, Winthrop had powerful friends in England. With their help, he received a charter in 1662. At this time, New Haven was made part of Connecticut. Both New Haven and Hartford served as colonial capitals.

The charter gave Connecticut more independence than most other English colonies in America. It spelled out the government for the colony, with a governor, twelve **magistrates,** and a general assembly. The assembly, which passed laws for the colony, could not have more than

Shipbuilding was at the heart of many of Connecticut's river towns. These towns experienced rapid growth as the industry became increasingly important through the mid-1600s and into the following century.

two members from any town. The king also said Connecticut's western border stretched to the "South Sea"—meaning the Pacific Ocean. Over time, however, Connecticut gave up its claim to those lands.

Happy with their charter, Connecticut residents focused on their daily activities. Most residents were farmers. Even merchants and skilled workers owned and worked their own farms. The best land was along the Connecticut River and smaller rivers. Important crops included corn, grains, **flax,** and tobacco. Farmers also raised cattle, pigs, and sheep. In the hilly regions away from the rivers, farmers had a more difficult time working the land, but they still managed to support their families. Some of the crops produced in the colony were sold to merchants in Boston, New York, and British colonies in the West Indies. Shipbuilding was an important early industry in towns along the Connecticut River and Long Island Sound.

Daily life in Connecticut was also shaped by religion. The first Puritan settlers always built a church as they created new towns. Their religion was eventually called Congregationalism. All residents were expected to go to church at least twice

20

a week. Some members of other churches also settled in Connecticut. But until the early 1700s, only Congregationalists were allowed to openly practice their religion.

By the 1680s, Connecticut faced a threat to its independence. England's King James II wanted more control over the New England colonies. He combined them into one region called the **Dominion** of New England. In 1686, the king named Edmond Andros the governor of the dominion. The next year, Andros came to Connecticut to assert his control. According to some reports, Connecticut leaders hid their charter in an oak tree in Hartford so Andros could not take it. This "Charter Oak" tree remains an important symbol of Connecticut's independence.

In reality, even without the charter Andros still ruled Connecticut, but the Dominion of New England did not last long. In 1689, King William III and Queen Mary came to power in England. When residents of Boston heard the news, they overthrew Andros and the other leaders named by James II. Their rebellion ended the dominion. The next month, Connecticut residents returned to their old government, as spelled out in the charter.

▸ Connecticut's Charter Oak appears on the back of the state commemorative quarter.

The Charter Oak survived until 1857, when a storm uprooted it. Afterward, people collected its acorns as mementos and used its wood to create miniature furniture, picture frames, and even a Colt revolver. The original Connecticut charter today is hung in a frame carved from the Charter Oak.

MANY ENGLISH COLONISTS IN AMERICA FEARED THAT SOME OF THEIR NEIGHBORS could be witches. In the 17th century, witches were thought to be the devil's helpers, and anyone found guilty of practicing witchcraft was killed. Most of the accused witches were women. Often, people accused neighbors they did not like of casting spells and performing other evil actions linked to witches.

The most famous witch trials in colonial times took place in Salem, Massachusetts, in 1692. Connecticut, though, had its own history of witch trials. The colony passed a law against witchcraft in 1642. About five years later, Windsor residents carried out New England's first known execution of an accused witch, Alice Young. Between 1648 and 1661, eight women and two of their husbands were executed as witches in Connecticut. Then in 1662 and 1663—around 30 years before Salem's Trials—the colony experienced a witchcraft panic. By

A Modeſt Enquiry Into the Nature of **Witchcraft,** AND How Perſons Guilty of that Crime may be *Convicted* : And the means uſed for their Diſcovery Diſcuſſed, both *Negatively* and *Affirmatively.* according to *SCRIPTURE* and *EXPERIENCE.*

By John Hale,

Paſtor of the Church of Chriſt in *Beverley,* Anno Domini 1 6 9 7.

When they ſay unto you, ſeek unto them that have Familiar Spirits and unto Wizzards,that peep,&c To the Law and to the Teſtimony ; if they ſpeak not according to this word, it is becauſe there is no light in them, Iſaiah VIII. 1 9, 20. *That which I ſee not teach thou me,* Job 3 4 32.

BOSTON in N. E. Printed by *B. Green,* and *J. Allen,* for *Benjamin Eliot* under the Town Houſe. 1702

the end of the panic, eight people, most of them from Hartford, had been brought to trial and three had been executed. Around the time of Salem's trials in 1692, seven women in Connecticut were accused of witchcraft. In 1697, the very last witchcraft trials in New England took place—in Connecticut, the site of the area's first trials. Both of the accused were found innocent.

Connecticut during the War

▶ The oldest American newspaper still being published is the *Hartford Courant.* It was established by Thomas Green in 1764. The newspaper won a Pulitzer Prize in 1999 for its coverage of breaking news.

DURING THE 18TH CENTURY, FRANCE AND GREAT Britain (which included England, Scotland, and Wales) competed to control North America. Starting in 1754, the two countries fought each other in the French and Indian War. When the fighting ended in 1763, the British had won control of Canada and lands in America east of the Mississippi River.

Connecticut, like the other American colonies, aided Great Britain during the war. The colony provided soldiers, and its farmers and merchants sold supplies to the British. Although the government had to raise taxes during the war, on the whole the colony's economy did well.

The British, however, were deeply in debt after the war. In 1763, **Parliament** began to pass laws that tightened its control over the colonies and taxed them to raise money. Until this time, Parliament had largely ignored the American colonies. For the next several years, into the early 1770s, many colonists tried to resist British attempts to collect taxes and limit their freedoms. These opponents of the new taxes were called Patriots. Colonists who supported Parliament and the king were called Loyalists. Connecticut, like several other colonies, had a large number of Loyalists and people who did not support either side. The Patriots, however, led the way to American independence.

The effort to protect American rights was centered in Boston. The American Revolution began outside that city on April 19, 1775, as British soldiers fought the Massachusetts **militia.** By the next day, Connecticut men were volunteering to go to Massachusetts and fight the British. One of the first was Israel Putnam. A farmer and tavern owner, Putnam had fought in the French and Indian War. At almost 60 years old, he led troops at the Battle of Bunker Hill.

Israel Putnam was a Connecticut farmer and tavern owner who led colonial troops at the Battle of Bunker Hill.

Throughout the American Revolution, Connecticut provided about 41,000 troops. The state also supplied ships to the navy. Its biggest role, however, was providing provisions. Connecticut's

David Bushnell's one-man Turtle submarine had a rather complicated design, as this diagram indicates. Though not very successful, it was the first submarine to dive and come back to the water's surface, and the first ever used as a warship.

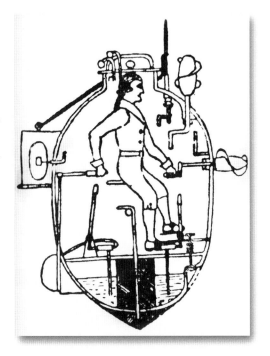

Jonathan Trumbull was the only colonial governor to openly support the Patriots. (His son Jonathan Jr. later won fame as an artist, painting pictures of George Washington and battle scenes from the Revolution.) Trumbull helped gather food, clothing, and equipment for the Continental army, which was led by General George Washington. The general and others sometimes called Connecticut the Provision State because of the large amount of supplies it provided.

In the early years of the war, several Connecticut natives played key roles for the Patriots. Benedict Arnold teamed up with Ethan Allen to take Fort Ticonderoga from the British. The British cannons captured at Ticonderoga helped the Patriots win a victory in Boston in 1776.

Also in 1776, David Bushnell built the first submarine used as a warship. His *Turtle* launched a sneak attack on a British ship docked in New York, but the mission failed. Another Connecticut resident made a daring mission for his country. Nathan Hale worked as a spy for General Washington in New York. He was caught by the British and executed for his activities. Before he died, Hale spoke these now-famous words: "I only regret that I have but one life to lose for my country."

For the most part, Connecticut escaped direct damage from the war. The only major battle took place in and around Danbury, in the western part of the state. In April 1777, British troops based in New York marched to Danbury. The British burned supplies and the homes of Patriots. In New York, Colonel Henry Ludington, the leader of a militia there, was told of the attack on Danbury. He needed to round up his troops, but he could not leave home. So his 16-year-old daughter, Sybil, volunteered for the task. She rode 40 miles (64 kilometers) through the night, gathering the men in her father's militia. The next morning, the militia marched to Danbury to confront the British. As the enemy troops tried to return to New York, they were attacked by soldiers led by Benedict Arnold. In the end, the British lost about 150

A statue of Nathan Hale in the Connecticut state capitol in Hartford.

Silas Deane is introduced to the famous French general, Lafayette.

Interesting Fact

▸ On October 1, 1985, Nathan Hale officially became Connecticut's State Hero.

troops, and they rarely attacked southern Connecticut again.

Although the British did not invade often, Connecticut residents along Long Island Sound remained on alert. The British had thousands of troops and many ships in New York. In May 1777, Jonathan Meigs led an American raid on British forces at Sag Harbor, Long Island. Sailing in small boats, about 400 Patriots destroyed 12 British warships, took 90 prisoners, and captured provisions. Not one of Meigs' soldiers died in the attack.

In 1774, the American colonists formed the Continental Congress to serve as their government. In 1776, after the Declaration of Independence was signed, the Second Continental Congress served as the first government of the new United States. The Connecticut representatives who signed the Declaration were Roger Sherman, Samuel Huntington, Oliver Wolcott, and William Williams.

Silas Deane had served in the Congress, but in 1776 he had a new job. Congress sent him to France to buy weapons and supplies for the Continental army. For a time, he worked with Benjamin Franklin and Arthur Lee, trying to convince the French government to aid the Americans.

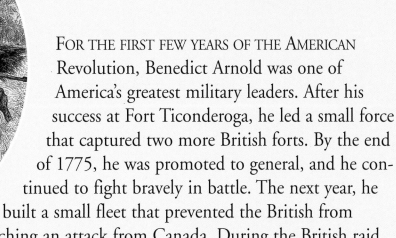

FOR THE FIRST FEW YEARS OF THE AMERICAN Revolution, Benedict Arnold was one of America's greatest military leaders. After his success at Fort Ticonderoga, he led a small force that captured two more British forts. By the end of 1775, he was promoted to general, and he continued to fight bravely in battle. The next year, he built a small fleet that prevented the British from launching an attack from Canada. During the British raid on Danbury in 1777, Arnold's horse was shot right underneath him, but Arnold continued to fight. Later in the year, he was severely wounded at the Battle of Saratoga, where he helped the Patriots earn a key victory.

Although eager to serve his country, Arnold often believed he was not given the respect he deserved. These feelings led Arnold to leave the Patriots and fight for the British. In 1781, he led a raid on his home state, attacking New London and Groton. After the war, Arnold lived in both Canada and England. Today, his name is still sometimes used to describe a person who is a traitor to the United States.

Chapter FIVE

After the War and Nationhood

This political cartoon shows the American victory in the Revolutionary War restoring the proper balance of liberty.

FOR CONNECTICUT RESIDENTS, VICTORY IN THE American Revolution meant they were part of a new, independent nation. The war had extra meaning for some of the state's 5,000 African-American slaves, because they received their freedom. In most cases, slaves won their freedom in return for joining the militia. In other cases, owners chose to let their slaves go. However, by 1790, Connecticut still had about 2,600 slaves, the most in New England. The state's slave population was small compared to the numbers in Southern states. Some Connecticut businesses had ties to the slave trade or relied on materials produced by Southern slaves.

After the war, Connecticut's businesses and government faced tough times. The state and many citizens were in debt, something that was happening all across New England. In 1786, some Massachusetts residents were not able to pay their taxes and debts. Led by Daniel Shays, the residents rebelled against their state's government. Connecticut leaders feared the violence of "Shays' Rebellion" would spread to their state, but no trouble broke out. Still, the rebellion and the huge debts convinced

Many businesses in Connecticut depended on materials produced by slave labor, such as the cotton grown on this southern plantation.

Like this blacksmith, many Americans were angry when their state governments demanded they pay taxes they couldn't afford. The mounting anger of many farmers and other workers was at the root of Shays' Rebellion.

many people in Connecticut and across the nation that the U.S. government had to change.

Starting in 1781, the U.S. government was based on the Articles of Confederation. This document let the states act almost as if they were separate countries. America lacked a strong central government. In 1787, all the states except Rhode Island sent **delegates** to Philadelphia to create a new central, or federal, government. The meeting was called the Constitutional Convention.

Connecticut's delegates were Roger Sherman, Oliver Ellsworth, and William Samuel Johnson. Sherman played an important role in Philadelphia. He helped arrange the "Connecticut Compromise." The large states and the small states disagreed on how many representa-

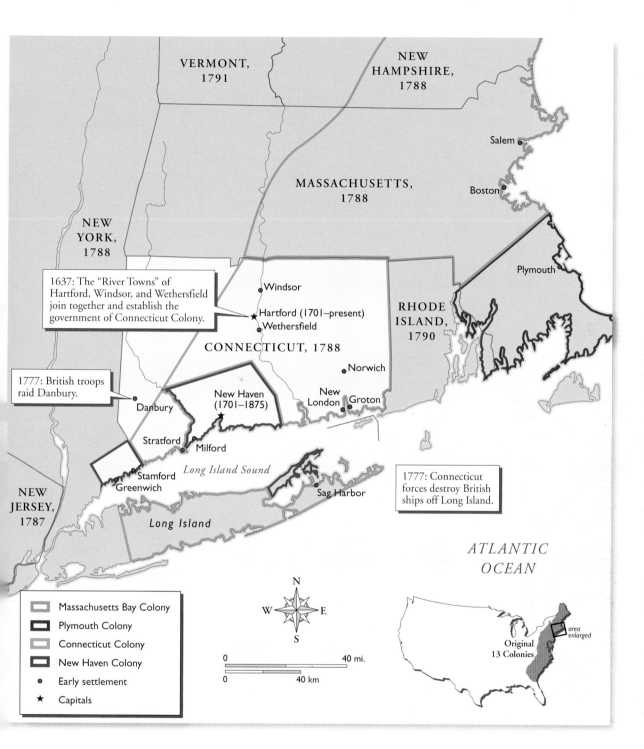

VERMONT,
1791

NEW
HAMPSHIRE,
1788

Salem

MASSACHUSETTS,
1788

Boston

NEW
YORK,
1788

Plymouth

1637: The "River Towns" of
Hartford, Windsor, and Wethersfield
join together and establish the
government of Connecticut Colony.

Windsor

Hartford (1701–present)
Wethersfield

RHODE
ISLAND,
1790

CONNECTICUT, 1788

Norwich

1777: British troops
raid Danbury.

New Haven
(1701–1875)

New
London Groton

Danbury

Stratford

Milford

Long Island Sound

1777: Connecticut
forces destroy British
ships off Long Island.

Stamford
Greenwich

NEW
JERSEY,
1787

Sag Harbor

Long Island

ATLANTIC
OCEAN

Massachusetts Bay Colony

Plymouth Colony

Connecticut Colony

New Haven Colony

Early settlement

Capitals

N
W   E
S

0   40 mi.

0   40 km

area
enlarged

Original
13 Colonies

tives each state would send to Congress. Large
states wanted the number of representatives to
reflect their large populations. Small states,

Connecticut Colony
before statehood

33

According to notes taken by James Madison at the Constitutional Convention, Roger Sherman made 138 speeches there to defend the rights of the small states such as Connecticut.

however, wanted equal representation. They were afraid that states with larger populations would have more power in the federal government because they would have more representatives. Sherman suggested that the number of House members should be based on a state's population, which pleased the large states. For the Senate, he said each state should have the same number of representatives, which pleased the small states. Sherman's compromise plan was included in the Constitution.

After the convention, Sherman and the other Connecticut delegates argued that the state should ratify, or accept, the new government. Johnson said, "Our national honour, once in so high esteem, is no more." The new federal government, he argued, would restore the nation's honor. On January 9, 1788, lawmakers meeting in Hartford voted 128–40 in favor of the Constitution. Connecticut was the fifth state to ratify the Constitution, which created the form of U.S. government still used today.

▸ The "Connecticut Compromise" sparked a debate over slavery during the Constitutional Convention. If, as Sherman suggested, the number of House members of each state was decided by state population, the southern states with large slave populations would have an advantage over the northern states. Finally, an infamous agreement was reached: each slave would count as only three-fifths of a person. For the most part, the problem of slavery was avoided in the Constitution. This is one reason the country remained divided over the issue and fought the Civil War.

The Old State House in Hartford preserves the memory of the patriots who helped to create the United States of America.

Circa 9000 B.C. The first Native Americans reach Connecticut.

1614 Dutch explorer Adriaen Block sails up the Connecticut River.

1633 The Dutch build a fort in Hartford; English settlers reach Windsor.

1636 Thomas Hooker leads a group of Puritans to Hartford.

1637 The English settlers and their Native American allies win the Pequot War.

1639 The Fundamental Orders describe the government of the Connecticut Colony.

1662 Connecticut receives a charter from King Charles II.

1687 To prevent Governor Edmond Andros from taking their charter, Connecticut residents hide it in a large oak tree.

1775 Benedict Arnold and Israel Putnam are two of the thousands of Connecticut residents who join the fighting against the British at the start of the American Revolution.

1776 Nathan Hale is executed for spying.

1777 British troops raid Danbury; Connecticut forces destroy British ships off Long Island.

1787 Roger Sherman's "Connecticut Compromise" becomes part of the Constitution.

1788 Connecticut becomes the fifth state to ratify the Constitution.

charter (CHAR-tuhr)
A charter is a document giving settlers permission to form and govern a colony. Colonists in Connecticut hid their charter in an oak tree.

constitution (kon-stuh-TOO-shun)
A constitution is a document outlining the structure of a government and a country's basic laws. Connecticut was the fifth state to ratify the constitution.

delegates (DEL-uh-gayts)
Delegates are people chosen to represent a group at a meeting. Delegates from Connecticut participated in the Continental Congress.

dominion (duh-MIN-yuhn)
A dominion is a region that is allowed to have some self-government but is still part of a larger country. King James II combined the New England colonies into the Dominion of New England.

flax (FLAKS)
Flax is a plant used to make the cloth linen. Flax was an important crop in colonial Connecticut.

fundamental (fun-duh-MEN-tuhl)
Something that is fundamental is basic or first. Some historians call the Fundamental Orders an early constitution.

magistrates (MADGE-uh-strayts)
Magistrates are elected officials who carry out laws. Connecticut's charter called for 12 magistrates to be part of the colony's government.

militia (muh-LISH-uh)
Members of a militia are volunteer soldiers who defend a town or state. Citizens of Connecticut joined the state's militia.

Parliament (PAR-luh-muhnt)
Parliament is the lawmaking body of Great Britain. Parliament passed laws that were unpopular with the colonists.

Protestant (PRAH-tiss-tuhnt)
Protestant religions are Christian religions that formed to protest practices of the Roman Catholic Church. The Puritans and Pilgrims were Protestant groups that settled in New England.

tribute (TRIB-yoot)
Tribute is money or goods paid from a weak government or tribe to a stronger one. Tribes near the Mohawk hunting grounds had to pay tribute to keep the peace.

Connecticut Colony's FOUNDING FATHERS

Andrew Adams (1736–1797)
Continental Congress delegate, 1777–82; Articles of Confederation signer; Connecticut supreme court justice, 1793–97

Oliver Ellsworth (1745–1807)
Continental Congress delegate, 1777–84; Constitutional Convention delegate, 1787; U.S. senator, 1789–96; Connecticut superior court justice, 1785–89; U.S. Supreme Court chief justice, 1796–1800

Titus Hosmer (1736–1780)
Continental Congress delegate, 1775–76, 1777–79; Articles of Confederation signer; U.S. senator, 1778–80

Samuel Huntington (1731–1796)
Continental Congress delegate, 1776–84; Declaration of Independence signer; Continental Congress president, 1779–81, 1783; Articles of Confederation signer; Connecticut lieutenant governor and superior court chief justice, 1784–86; Connecticut governor, 1786–1796

William Samuel Johnson (1727–1819)
Connecticut legislature member, 1761–66, 1771–1775; Elected to First Continental Congress (but due to divided loyalties refused to participate), 1774; Congress of Confederation delegate, 1784–87; Continental Congress delegate, 1785–87; Constitutional Convention delegate, 1787; U.S. Constitution signer; U.S. senator, 1789–91

Roger Sherman (1721–1793)
Connecticut legislature member, 1755, 1756, 1758–61, 1764–66; Connecticut senator, 1766–85; Connecticut superior court justice, 1766, 1767, 1773–88; Articles of Association signer; Continental Congress delegate, 1774–81, 1783, 1784; Declaration of Independence signer; Constitutional Convention distinguished member, 1787; Articles of Confederation signer and drafter; U.S. Constitution signer; U.S. House of Representatives, 1789–91; U.S. senator, 1791–93; Only person to sign all four historical documents

William Williams (1731–1811)
Continental Congress delegate, 1776–78, 1783, 1784; Declaration of Independence signer

Oliver Wolcott (1726–1797)
Continental Congress delegate, 1775–78, 1780–84; Declaration of Independence signer; Articles of Confederation signer; Connecticut lieutenant governor, 1787–96; Connecticut governor, 1796–97

For Further INFORMATION

Web Sites

Visit our homepage for lots of links about the Connecticut colony:
http://www.childsworld.com/links.html

Note to Parents, Teachers, and Librarians:
We routinely verify our Web links to make sure they're safe,
active sites—so encourage your readers to check them out!

Books

Bober, Natalie. *Countdown to Independence: A Revolution of Ideas in England and Her Colonies, 1760–1776.* New York: Atheneum Books for Young Readers, 2001.

Doherty, Kiernan. *Puritans, Pilgrims, and Merchants: Founders of the Northeastern Colonies.* Minneapolis: Oliver Press, 1999.

Girod, Christina M. *The Thirteen Colonies: Connecticut.* San Diego: Lucent Books, 2002.

Newman, Shirlee Petkin. *The Pequots.* Danbury, Conn.: Franklin Watts, 2000.

Quiri, Patricia Ryon. *The Algonquians.* New York: Franklin Watts, 1992.

Places to Visit or Contact

Connecticut Historical Society
For more information about Connecticut and its history
One Elizabeth Street
Hartford, CT 06105
860/236-5621

Museum of Connecticut History
To see the Fundamental Orders, 1662 charter, and other important items from Connecticut's past
Connecticut State Library
231 Capitol Avenue
Hartford, CT 06106
860/757-6535

Index

About the Author

MICHAEL BURGAN IS A FREELANCE WRITER OF BOOKS FOR CHILDREN and adults. A history graduate of the University of Connecticut, he has written more than 60 fiction and nonfiction children's books for various publishers. For adult audiences, he has written news articles, essays, and plays. Michael Burgan is a recipient of an Edpress Award and belongs to the Society of Children's Book Writers and Illustrators.